KID GUARDIANS®
JUST BE SAFE™
SERIES

I Always Wear My Helmet

by
Diane H. Pappas
& Richard D. Covey

Illustrated by
Ric Estrada

SCHOLASTIC INC.
New York Toronto London Auckland Sydney
Mexico City New Delhi Hong Kong Buenos Aires

To Our Special Kid Guardians with love — John, Casey, and Nikos
— D.H.P. & R.D.C.

To my wife, Loretta, and our children, Aaron, Marc, Aleli, Rebekah,
Seth, Jeremy, Ethan, Hannah, and of course Zilia, and their
spouses and children with love
— R. E.

Thanks to the artists of The Pixel Factory (special thanks to Desma & Bob)
for contributing their talents to the creative production of these books.

———————————————

ISBN 0-439-88031-9

Printed in the U.S.A.
First printing, September 2006

MEET THE KID GUARDIANS®

From their home base in the mystical Himalayan mountain kingdom of Shambala, Zak the Yak and the Kid Guardians® are always on alert, ready to protect the children of the world from danger.

 ZAK THE YAK is a gentle giant with a heart of gold. He's the leader of the Kid Guardians®.

 Loyal and lovable, **SCRUBBER** is Zak's best friend and sidekick.

 BUZZER is both street-smart and book-smart and not afraid to show off.

 Always curious about the world, **SMOOCH** loves to meet new people and see new places.

 CARROT is full of energy and the first to jump in when help is needed.

 Whenever a child is in danger, the **TROUBLE BUBBLE**™ sounds an alarm and then instantly transports the Kid Guardians® to that location.

It was the day of the town bike race.

"Hi! I want to enter the race," Pablo told the man at the sign-up table.

"Do you have your helmet?" asked the man.
"I don't need a helmet," said Pablo. "I am an excellent rider!"

"Uh-oh! Trouble ahead!" called Zak. "Come on, Buzzer, let's go!"

Zak and Buzzer arrive to offer Pablo their help.
"Pablo, you must always wear a helmet when you ride your bike,"
said Zak. "Even good riders have accidents."

"Helmets are also important when you skate, ride a scooter, or ride a skateboard," added Buzzer.

"Wow, Zak—this red helmet is cool!" said Pablo, gratefully.

"And Pablo, the helmet must fit you correctly," Zak pointed out.

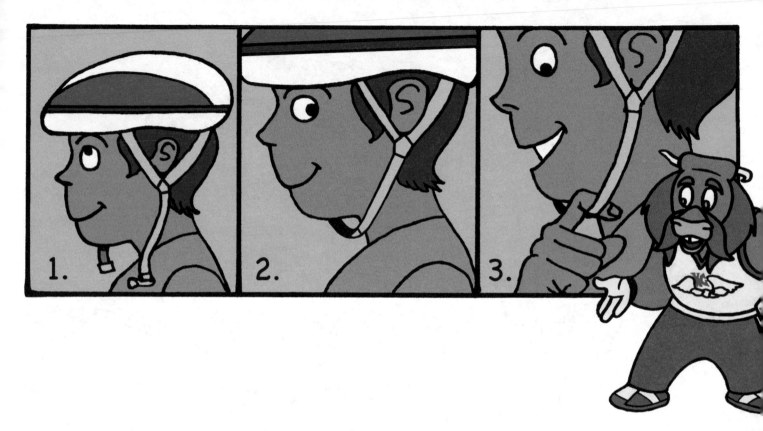

Zak then told Pablo about the three rules of helmet safety:

1. The helmet should sit low and snug on your head.
2. The "V" strap should touch the bottom of each ear.
3. The chinstrap should be tight against your chin, with only one finger of distance.

"Shake your head to make sure your helmet will not jiggle or move," added Buzzer.

"Wearing bright clothes helps drivers and other riders see you," added Zak.

"Ready . . . set . . . GO!"

"It looks like it's going to be a safe race," said Zak.

"Well," said Jill to Pablo, "we didn't win, but we had fun."
"And we were safe!" added Pablo.

Let's remember what you learned about bicycle safety:

1. Always wear a helmet when you skate or ride a bike, a scooter, or a skateboard.
2. Make sure your helmet fits properly.
3. Wear bright clothing so drivers can see you.